… INFLUENTIAL …

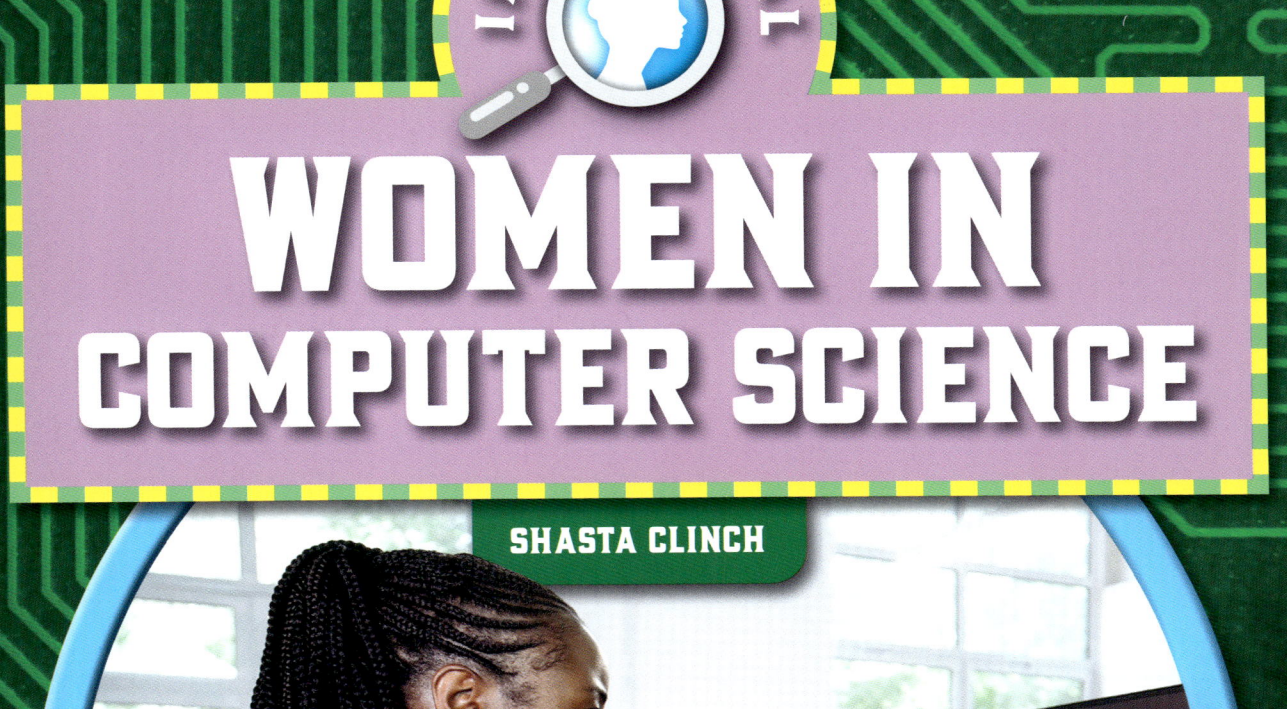

WOMEN IN COMPUTER SCIENCE

SHASTA CLINCH

childsworld.com

The Child's World®
childsworld.com

Published by The Child's World®
800-599-READ • www.childsworld.com

Copyright © 2025 by The Child's World®
All rights reserved. No part of this book may be reproduced or utilized in any form or by any means without written permission from the publisher.

Photography Credits
Photographs ©: Andrey Popov/Shutterstock Images, cover (programmer), 1 (programmer); Kovalchuk Oleksandr/Shutterstock Images, cover (background), 1 (background), 3 (background); Alexander Skowalsky/Noun Project, cover (icon), 1 (icon), 3 (icon), back cover; Alfred Edward Chalon/A. Stirling/Science Museum Group, 5; Photo 12 Collection/Alamy, 6, 22; James S. Davis/US Navy, 9; Lio Putra/Shutterstock Images, 10 (top left); Shutterstock Images, 10 (top right), 10 (bottom); NASA, 13, 14; Ken Wolter/Shutterstock Images, 16–17; R. Farrell/ITU Pictures, 19; Steve Jurvetson/Flickr, 20

ISBN Information
9781503889569 (Reinforced Library Binding)
9781503890251 (Portable Document Format)
9781503891494 (Online Multi-user eBook)
9781503892736 (Electronic Publication)

LCCN 2023950448

Printed in the United States of America

Shasta Clinch is a freelance copy editor and proofreader. She lives with her husband and two lovely littles in New Jersey.

TABLE OF CONTENTS

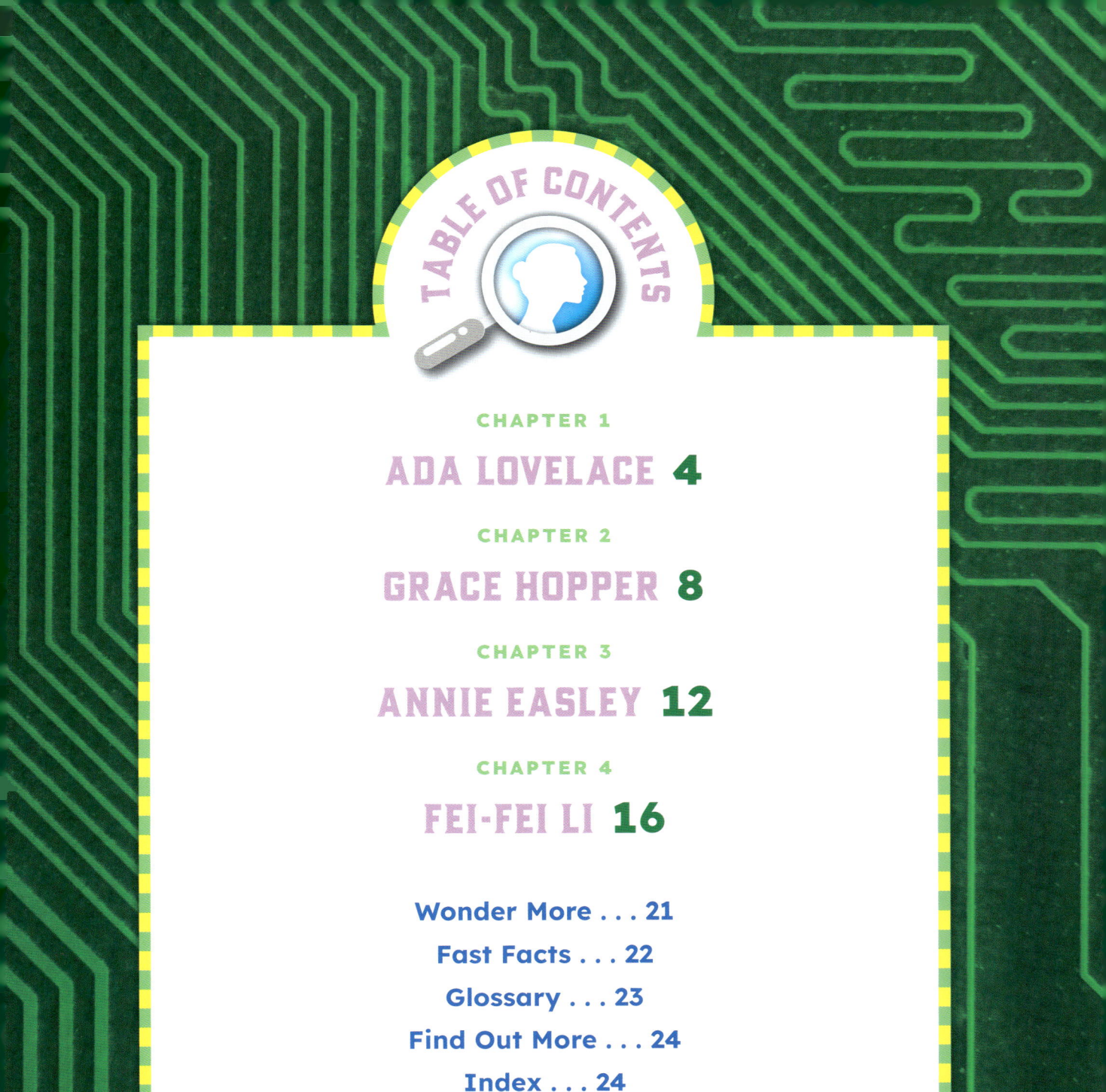

CHAPTER 1
ADA LOVELACE 4

CHAPTER 2
GRACE HOPPER 8

CHAPTER 3
ANNIE EASLEY 12

CHAPTER 4
FEI-FEI LI 16

Wonder More . . . 21
Fast Facts . . . 22
Glossary . . . 23
Find Out More . . . 24
Index . . . 24

CHAPTER 1

ADA LOVELACE

On December 10, 1815, Ada Lovelace was born in London, England. She was the daughter of the famous poet Lord Byron. Her mother was Annabella Byron. Lovelace's parents separated soon after she was born. She never got to know her father.

In Lovelace's time, girls were raised to become wives and mothers. Boys were taught subjects that would help in jobs outside the home. Girls were not taught the same things that boys were.

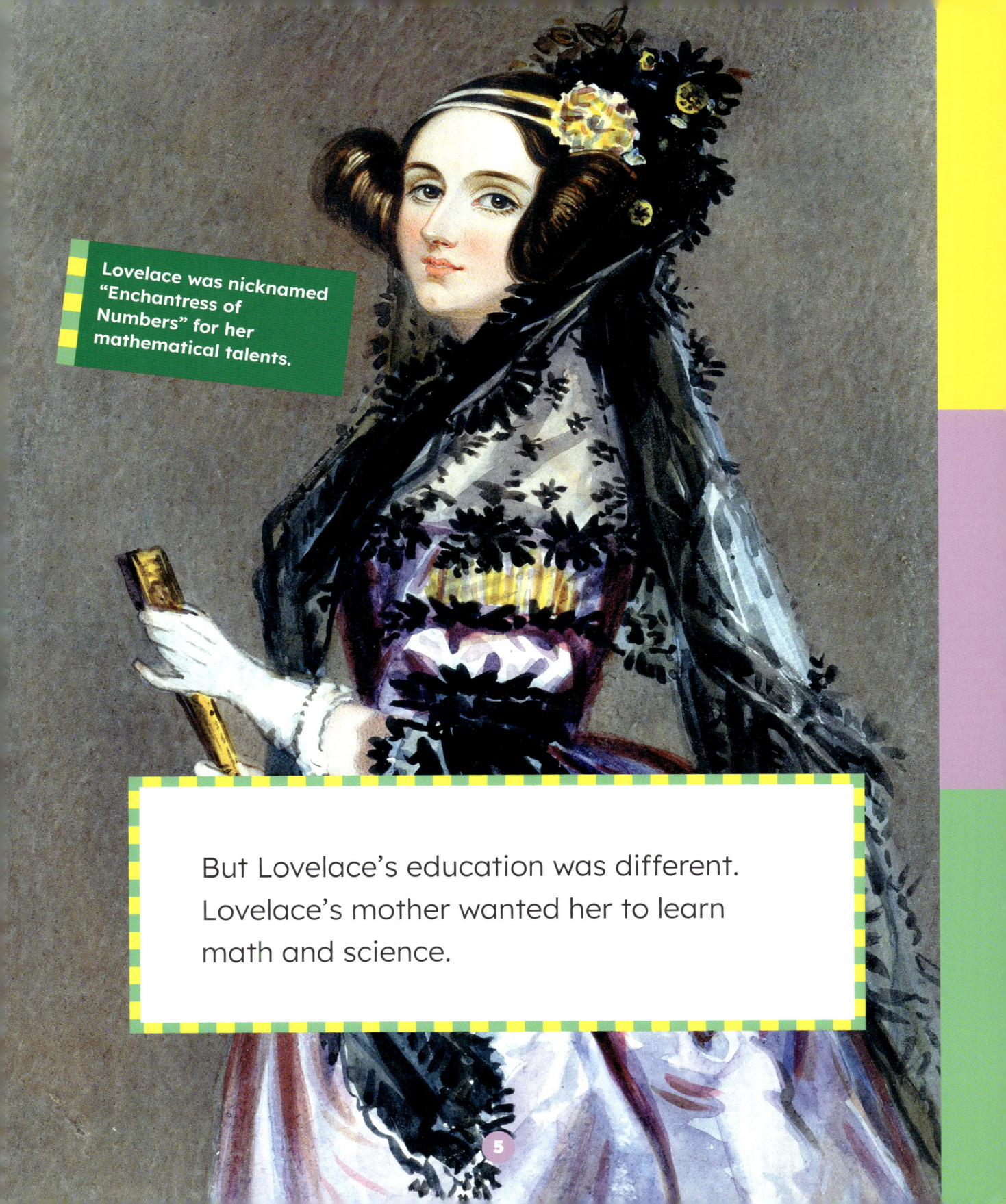

Lovelace was nicknamed "Enchantress of Numbers" for her mathematical talents.

But Lovelace's education was different. Lovelace's mother wanted her to learn math and science.

Babbage built part of the Analytical Engine but died before he could finish it.

When Lovelace was 17, she met Charles Babbage. He was a math professor. He had an idea for a machine called the **Analytical** Engine. It would be able to add, subtract, multiply, and divide numbers. It is considered to be the first computer.

In 1843, Lovelace **translated** a report written in French about the machine. But she also added her own notes. In the notes, she described an **algorithm** for the machine. This algorithm would use the computer to solve a complicated math problem. It is considered to be the first computer program. Lovelace wondered whether computers would be able to work with letters and symbols, too.

Ada Lovelace died in 1852. Her contributions to computer science were not understood for another 100 years. In 2009, Ada Lovelace Day was created to celebrate women in science.

CHAPTER 2

GRACE HOPPER

Grace Hopper was born in New York City in 1906. Her mother loved studying mathematics. She passed that love to her daughter. Hopper went to college and became a math professor. But when the United States joined World War II (1939–1945), Hopper wanted to help. She joined the navy in 1943. She worked on an early version of today's computers. Hopper and her team made top-secret **calculations** that helped the United States in the war.

Hopper served in the US Navy for 43 years.

HOW A COMPUTER PROGRAM WORKS

Programming languages are made to be understood by people. Computers only understand code in sequences of zeros and ones known as binary.

A programmer writes code in a programming language.

00101011
01101010
101110101
11011000
10100110

The computer translates the code to binary, a language it can understand.

The computer follows the code's instructions.

After the war ended, Hopper continued working with computers. She learned how to program them. Programmers write code to give a computer instructions. At the time, programmers wrote code that computers could read. But it was hard for most people to understand. In 1956, Hopper designed a programming language that used instructions written in English. This allowed more people to access computers and learn to write programs.

After Hopper left the navy, she worked for a computer company. She also taught classes and gave presentations. She passed her knowledge down to new **generations** of programmers. She believed this was her biggest accomplishment. Hopper continued to work and teach until she died in 1992.

CHAPTER 3

ANNIE EASLEY

On April 23, 1933, Annie Easley was born. She grew up in Birmingham, Alabama. Easley studied to become a pharmacist. A pharmacist is a person who prepares and provides medicine. In 1954, she married her husband. They moved to Cleveland, Ohio. She decided to look for other jobs.

One day in 1955, she read in a newspaper about the National Advisory Committee for Aeronautics (NACA). She applied for a job there. She would have to solve, or compute, math problems by hand. She had always been good at math. Two weeks later, Easley had the job. She was now a computer.

WHEN COMPUTERS WERE PEOPLE

The earliest human computers were often women or people of color. Their work was not properly respected for many years. That began to change in the 2010s. A 2016 book called *Hidden Figures* told the story of early computers. The book was made into a movie that same year.

Easley worked at NASA for 34 years.

Easley's work at NASA helped support the 1997 rocket launch that sent a spacecraft to the planet Saturn.

Eventually, machines could solve certain math problems. The word *computer* began to refer to machines instead of people. Easley became a scientist who worked with these machines. She learned how to write computer code. NACA became the National Aeronautics and Space Administration (NASA). Easley's code helped launch rockets.

Easley was one of the first Black women to work for NASA. She worked hard to make it easier for other women and people of color to work there, too. Easley's mother always told her she could become anything she wanted to be. And she did.

CHAPTER 4

FEI-FEI LI

Artificial intelligence (AI) is an area of computer science. It involves using computers to solve problems that usually require human intelligence. An important part of teaching computers to solve these problems is giving them the right **data**. If a computer gets the wrong data, what it learns might be incorrect.

The Stanford Artificial Intelligence Laboratory is located in this building on Stanford University's campus in California.

Computer scientist Fei-Fei Li wanted to make sure computers got the right data. She created a large collection of pictures called ImageNet. She realized that if computers had only a few pictures of an object, then they would only understand those versions of the object. Li's collection includes thousands of pictures of many items. This gives computers a more complete sense of an object. This way, computers can get a clearer picture of the world.

Li became a professor of computer science at Stanford University in 2009.

Li cofounded the Stanford Human-Centered AI Institute in 2019 to work on making sure AI benefits people.

Computers are taught by humans. Humans have **biases**. Li realized this and understood that computers could learn these biases, too. To fix this problem, the computer scientists who taught computers needed to be more diverse. Li has tried to get more women and people of color working on AI. She has also worked with lawmakers about AI. In 2018, she spoke to members of the US Congress. She talked about the importance of using AI safely.

WONDER MORE

Wondering about New Information
How much did you know about women in computer science before reading this book? What new information did you learn? Write down three facts that this book taught you. Was the new information surprising? Why or why not?

Wondering How It Matters
What is one way computer science relates to your life? If you cannot think of a personal connection, imagine a way the topic might affect other kids. What impact might it have on their lives?

Wondering Why
AI is becoming more important in people's everyday lives. Why do you think it is important for AI to be fair? Do you think it helps the world as a whole?

Ways to Keep Wondering
Computer science is a complex topic. After reading this book, what questions do you have about this science? Is there a part of computer science that interests you?

FAST FACTS

- Ada Lovelace and Charles Babbage worked together.

- Babbage designed the first computer.

- Lovelace wrote the first computer program.

- Grace Hopper joined the US Navy during World War II. She used her math skills to help the war effort.

- Hopper created a programming language that used English. It was easier to understand than older computer languages.

- Annie Easley was a human computer before she became a computer scientist.

- Easley worked for NACA and NASA.

- Fei-Fei Li works on AI.

- Li created ImageNet as a new way for computers to learn.

GLOSSARY

algorithm (AL-guh-rith-um) An algorithm is step-by-step instructions to solve a problem or complete a task. Ada Lovelace wrote an algorithm that is considered to be the first computer program.

analytical (an-uh-LI-tih-kul) Being analytical means being able to carefully study the parts of something to learn more about the whole. Charles Babbage designed a computer he called the Analytical Engine.

biases (BY-uh-suhz) Biases are unfair opinions about something or someone. Fei-Fei Li is concerned about the effects human biases have on AI.

calculations (kal-kyoo-LAY-shuns) Calculations are mathematical ways of solving a problem to get an answer. Grace Hopper performed calculations in her job with the US Navy.

data (DAY-tuh) Data are information used for some purpose. Some AI programs use data given to them by people to solve problems.

generations (jeh-nur-AY-shuns) Generations are groups of people who were born around the same time. Teachers help the next generations learn.

translated (TRANZ-lay-ted) When someone has translated something, she has changed its words from one language into another. Ada Lovelace translated a French article about the Analytical Engine into English.

FIND OUT MORE

In the Library

Calvert, Jennifer. *Science Superstars: 30 Brilliant Women Who Changed the World*. New York, NY: Castle Point Books, 2021.

Jeapes, Ben. *Ada Lovelace*. New York, NY: Abrams Books, 2020.

Marquardt, Meg. *What is Coding?* Parker, CO: The Child's World, 2020.

On the Web

Visit our website for links about women in computer science:

childsworld.com/links

Note to Parents, Caregivers, Teachers, and Librarians: We routinely verify our web links to make sure they are safe and active sites. So encourage your readers to check them out!

INDEX

AI, 16–20
algorithms, 7
Analytical Engine, 6–7

Babbage, Charles, 6
biases, 20
binary, 10

code, 10–11, 15
computer programs, 7, 10, 11

Easley, Annie, 12–15

Hopper, Grace, 8–11

Li, Fei-Fei, 16–20
Lovelace, Ada, 4–7

NACA, 12, 15
NASA, 13–15

World War II, 8